'The Missing Oblation':

The Contents of
the Early Antiochene Anaphora

edited by John R. K. Fenwick

*Assistant Secretary for Ecumenical Affairs,
to the Archbishop of Canterbury*

THE ALCUIN CLUB and the GROUP FOR RENEWAL OF WORSHIP (GROW)

The Alcuin Club, which exists to promote the study of Christian liturgy in general and of Anglican liturgy in particular, traditionally published a single volume annually for its members. This ceased in 1986. Similarly, GROW was responsible from 1975 to 1986 for the quarterly 'Grove Liturgical Studies'. Since the beginning of 1987 the two have sponsored a Joint Editorial Board to produce quarterly 'Joint Liturgical Studies'. Full details of the previous publications and the current series of Joint Liturgical Studies are set out in the end-pages of this Study.

THE COVER PICTURE

is of an Icon of St. John Chrysostom

First Impression December 1989
ISSN 0951-2667
ISBN 1 85174 127 5

GROVE BOOKS LIMITED
Bramcote   Nottingham   NG9 3DS

CONTENTS

NOTE RE THE TWO PARTS AND THE TABLES

The Tables are a point of reference in both Parts of this Study, though they are printed within Part 2. The alphabetical listing in the headings to the Tables is used consistently for the same features of the Anaphora (and 'A' is the Preface and 'B' the Pre-Sanctus), and is found in the headings to the sub-sections of each Part (e.g., '1C' is the sub-section of Part 1 handling the Post-Sanctus.

The publishers regret the very small size of the print in the Tables, which was necessitated by the five- and six-column form of presentation. The ability to read along one horizontal line for five (or even six) texts was considered the over-riding priority, even if that entails the use of magnification for many readers.

ABBREVIATIONS

OC   Oriens Christianus.
OCP   Orientalia Christiana Periodica
OS   L'Orient Syrien
PEER R. Jasper and G. Cuming (ed.), *Prayers of the Eucharist, Early and Reformed,* Oxford
      OUP, (2nd ed., London and New York)

Due to technical reasons the Greek text is reproduced without accents or breathings. The original Mss were of course in uncials.

Introduction

The purpose of the present Study is to present evidence to support the claim that the anaphora of the Twelve Apostles (ATA), the anaphora of the Liturgy of John Chrysostom (LJC) and Apostolic Constitutions (AC) are all independent derivatives of a single prayer. It will be argued that the prayer (which must have claim to considerable antiquity and be of great significance in determining the development of the Antiochene liturgical tradition) has been subject to various degrees of conflation, influence and reworking to produce the three anaphoras in the form that we now have them.

For the sake of clarity this argument is presented in two parts. The first deals with the relationship between ATA and LJC, which has been long acknowledged. Tables showing the texts in parallel are presented for each section of the anaphora and are then commented upon. The second part then brings AC into consideration, concentrating particularly on the areas of the anaphora which are common to LJC and ATA and are therefore likely to be from the common original. Once again, each section of the anaphora is reviewed in turn and tentative conclusions drawn from the results.

The Study not only opens up further the whole area of prayer construction in the fourth and fifth centuries, but comes to the conclusion that the parent anaphora lacked any oblation or offering of the eucharistic elements to God (hence the title of the Study). Such a conclusion clearly has important implications for our understanding of the eucharist both in antiquity and today.

Part I

THE ANAPHORAS OF THE TWELVE APOSTLES AND OF THE LITURGY OF JOHN CHRYSOSTOM

The relationship between the so-called 'Anaphora of the Twelve Apostles' and that found in the Liturgy attributed to St John Chrysostom remains one of those areas of liturgical investigation that has not yet been satisfactorily tidied up. That there is a relationship seems to have been accepted at least since 1920 when Patriarch Ignatios Ephrem II Rahmani drew attention to the large amount of material shared between them.[1]

In 1937 Hieronymus Engberding published the two anaphoral texts in parallel columns together with the text of two Maronite MSS.[2]

After a characteristically detailed examination of the texts, Engberding reached a number of conclusions, including:

a) that the Syro-Antiochene text of ATA is the most important aid so far discovered to tracing the history of LJC.

b) that the ATA version of the Preface is probably the original form, and that its brevity and theological simplicity point to a date in the 4th century for the Greek original.

c) that the home of the anaphora is almost certainly Antioch.

Over twenty years later Raes and Khouri-Sarkis independently agreed with Engberding's conclusions.[3]

The only significant dissentient voice seems to be that of Georg Wagner who briefly considered the text of ATA in his study on the sources of LJC.[4]

He questioned the assumption that the shorter of two similar texts is necessarily the older, and on the strength of this prefered to conclude that ATA was more likely to represent an abbreviation of LJC than its parent form. He thus dismissed any possibility that ATA could be an independent witness to the original version of LJC. The source, date and relationship of the two anaphoras is therefore once again, in the words of Jasper and Cuming, 'open to debate'.[5]

Throughout the various discussions of the anaphoras there constantly recur references to two other eucharistic prayers—that of St Basil in its Byzantine form (Byz-Basil) and the Syrian recension of the Liturgy of St James (Sy-Jas). It is

---

[1] I. E. Rahmani, *Fasti della Chiesa Patriarcale Antiochena*, (Rome, 1920), XXVI-XXXI).

[2] H. Engberding, 'Die syrische Anaphora der zwolf Apostel und ihre Paralleltexte', in OC 7(1937)213-247, hereafter cited as zwolf.

[3] A. Raes, 'L'authenticite de la Liturgie byzantine de S. Jean Chrysostome' in OCP 24(1958)5-16; G.Khouri-Sarkis, 'L'Origene syrienne de l'anaphore byzantine de saint Jean Chrysostom' in OS 7(1962)3-68).

[4] G. Wagner, *Der Ursprung der Chrysostomusliturgie*, LQF 59, (Munster, 1973), pp.43-51, cited as *Ursprung.*.

[5] PEER p.93.

widely acknowledged that at various points LJC bears clear signs of having been influenced by Byz-Basil and ATA by Sy-Jas. However there has been no systematic examination of the precise extent and nature of the influence.

The present writer has already put forward a case for concluding that in the late fourth century at least it was possible to conflate independent anaphoras, particularly where a prayer was increasingly felt to be deficient in one or more areas.[1] A summary of the argument and conclusions, with an example of the method used, has already been published in the series preceding the present one.[2] This section of the present paper therefore attempts to explore the hypothesis that the differences between ATA and LJC are due to the fact that a common original has been independently conflated in various degrees with Sy-Jas and Byz-Basil.[3]

SOURCES AND METHODOLOGY
The following are the sources of the main texts used:
ATA—A.Raes, 'Anaphora syriaca Duodecim Apostolorum prima' in idem, *Anaphorae Syriacae*, I,215-223, Rome, 1939.
LJC—F.Brightman, *Liturgies Eastern and Western* 321-337, Oxford, 1896.
Sy-Jas—O. Heiming, *Anaphorae Syriacae, II*, 141-171, Rome, 1953.
Gr-Jas—B.C.Mercier, *'La liturgie de saint Jacques' in Patrologia Orientalis*, 26 (1946) 115-256.
Byz-Basil—F.Brightman, *Liturgies Eastern and Western* 321-337.
   In order to avoid repeatedly qualifying statements, the argument is pursued as though the hypothesis being tested were in fact true.

---

[1] 'An Investigation into the Common Origin of the Anaphoras of the Liturgies of St Basil and St James', PhD Thesis, London, 1985 (hereinafter cited as *Investigation*), to be published by the Pontifical Institute for Oriental Studies in the series Orientalia Christiana Analecta.

[2] John Fenwick, *Fourth Century Anaphoral Construction Techniques* (Grove Liturgical Study no. 45, 1986).

[3] In August 1989 Robert Taft presented a paper at the York Congress of *Societas Liturgica* ('The Authenticity of the Chrysostom Anaphora Revisited'—cited as *Authenticity*) in which he makes precisely this assumption. Taft's paper is an attempt to identify by computer analysis material in LJC which may confidently be attributed to St. John Chrysostom himself. Its results are impressive, but are unfortunately limited to the Preface.

1A PREFACE

As Engberding noted[1] a significant portion of the Preface (AB33-41) is identical in both ATA and LJC. This material is not found at all in either Sy-Jas or Byz-Basil and therefore must clearly belong to the common ancestral form. The preceding material is somewhat more problematic. Engberding is confident only of the *Axion kai dikaion*, though he thought it likely that the *soi eucharistein* of LJC was part of the common original, on the grounds that it was almost certainly the original verb in primitive anaphoras. It should be noted however, that the Sahidic version of the Basiline anaphora (ES-Basil[2]) also lacks the verb and Engberding's assumption should perhaps be treated with caution (especially since the words *eucharistoumen soi* are found later in the Preface (AB46)—might not this be the original position?). Sy-Jas has *tibi gratias agere:* if ATA did at an early stage acquire it from that source, it must have independently lost it again.

Engberding is even more cautious about the remaining praise-verbs, pointing to their relative fluidity in ancient anaphoras.[3] It is worth noting that Sy-Jas and Byz-Basil are much fuller than ATA and LJC at this point, suggesting their later date and mutual influence (for which we have argued elsewhere).[4]

Both ATA and LJC retain a Trinitarian address to God (AB14-20), somewhat expanded in LJC. Taft's computer analysis suggests that this expansion (especially AB15-16) may have been made by John Chrysostom himself, which raises intriguing possibilities about the Saint's relationship with the original anaphora, the Trinitarian address itself might normally be expected to be a secondary elaboration, perhaps in imitation of AB40-41, but its presence in both anaphoras suggests that it would be wrong to rule out the possibility of its having been in the original text. Certainly neither is likely to have derived it from Sy-Jas or Byz-Basil. The latter does have a Trinitarian theme in AB50ff., but it is of a highly elaborated nature and unlikely to have been abbreviated to the simple AB14-20.

LJC then has a further expression of thanksgiving, not found in ATA (AB42-47) which has the appearance of an ancient ending.

There are no discernible links here with Byz-Basil, therefore suggesting an independent development relating to the specific liturgy being celebrated, a trend noted by Bobrinskoy.[5]

The evidence afforded by the Preface is clearly insufficient to support the hypothesis that the common ancestor of ATA and LJC has been independently assimilated to Sy-Jas and Byz-Basil respectively. The praise-verbs certainly point to external influence, which *could* have come from those sources, but it is impossible to assert this with any confidence.

---

[1] Zwolf, p.216.

[2] See Fenwick, *Investigation* (p.9) for an explanation of the nomenclature used here. The text may be found in J. Doresse and E. Lanne *'Une Témoir archaique de la liturgie coptic de S. Basile,* Louvain, 1960.

[3] Zwolf, p.236.

[4] Fenwick, *op. cit.*.

[5] 'Liturgie et ecclesiologia trinitaire de S. Basil' in *Verbum Cora* 23 (89) (1969) 1-32

1B PRE-SANCTUS

The Pre-Sanctus in ATA begins rather abruptly (*Ante te enim stant in circuitu . . .*), with no apparent attempt to link it with the preceding material. Engberding is inclined to see this as a mark of its primitive status, pointing out that the linking section in LJC shows signs of a later, more developed style.[1] Wagner, on the other hand, sees the omission of AB43ff., by ATA as a sign of 'somewhat clumsy abbreviation' on the part of the Syrian editor.[2] Wagner does not, however, take into account two significant facts: firstly, that an abrupt beginning to the Pre-Sanctus is found in a number of anaphoras (ES-Basil, for example) where it is generally accepted as an indication of antiquity; and, secondly, that even in LJC the link is in effect only provided by the word *kaitoi*—the continuity of thought is nothing like as smooth as in Sy-Jas.

Far from being a 'clumsy abbreviation', the Pre-Sanctus of ATA may contain clues concerning the evolution of the anaphora. As Engberding noted the Preface of ATA comprises a completely self-contained prayer, possessing in concise form: Address to God, Thanksgiving for Creation and Redemption, and a summarising doxology naming the three Persons of the Trinity[3]. The whole section surely has a strong claim to be considered as one of Cuming's 'mini-anaphoras'.[4]

If the classic anaphoras were indeed built up by the addition of a series of sections to the primitive core, then the relative discontinuity of thought between Preface and Pre-Sanctus in ATA should pose no difficulty. AB46f. in LJC then looks very much like a later Redactor's attempt to improve the flow.

Turning to the actual text, a number of features are immediately obvious:

a) Sy-Jas commences with a list of heavenly bodies (derived from the old Jerusalem anaphora) which are not found in any of the other prayers under review here.

b) Sy-Jas and Byz-Basil share two pairs of beings (AB60-62) not found in ATA or LJC. The likelihood of mutual influence here has been discussed elsewhere.[5]

c) Both Sy-Jas and Byz-Basil contain an embolism, derived in the main from the text of Scripture, describing the Seraphim (AB69-78). The latter part of this (AB77-78) is found in ATA, presumably under the influence of Sy-Jas.

Once such probable secondary material is identified, it can be seen that the Pre-Sanctus material common to ATA and LJC consists of a relatively brief naming of the Cherubim and Seraphim (though the archangels and angels of LJC (AB59) are slightly problematic—they do not look like a straight borrowing from Byz-Basil—Engberding seems to suspect influence from Daniel 7.10.[6]

Engberding draws attention to the way in which both the Cherubim and Seraphim are designated *exapteryga polyommata*, in contravention of Scriptural

---

[1] Zwolf, p.238f.
[2] Ursprung, p.47.
[3] Zwolf, p.241.
[4] G. J. Cuming 'Some very early Anaphoras' in *Worship* 58.2 (March 1989), pp.168-172.
[5] *Investigation, passim.*
[6] Zwolf, p.240.

text and prevailing usage, but does not argue strongly for its being the original form.

The Barberini MS ends the Pre-Sanctus of LJC with the single verb *adonta*, which would seem to have a strong claim to originality in view of the almost universal tendency to elaborate and standardize this section (no doubt due in large measure to its function as a 'cue' to the Sanctus). ATA follows Sy-Jas here, and later MSS of LJC agree with Byz-Basil.

Thus the Pre-Sanctus also shows ATA and LJC preserving a common simplicity by comparison with Sy-Jas and Byz-Basil. LJC indeed may preserve the original form, while ATA shows increasing signs of 'Syrianization'

1C POST-SANCTUS

Here too, ATA and LJC exhibit a common brevity by comparison with Sy-Jas and Byz-Basil. This section comprises a relatively simple further ascription of holiness to the Trinity, followed by a quotation of John 3.16 as an introduction to the Institution Narrative. The other two anaphoras by contrast have lengthy accounts of the Fall and Redemption, ending with the earthly ministry of Christ in the case of Sy-Jas, but continuing to the Second Coming in Byz-Basil. The difference between the two groups of prayers is striking, and deserves some attempt at explanation.

We have already drawn attention to the fact that the primitive Jerusalem anaphora contained very little Christological/Redemption material and that this was very likely imported into the amplified version of the prayer (which we now know as Jas) by the wholesale borrowing of the Basiline Post-Sanctus.[1] But even the Preface of the original form of the Basiline anaphora (as witnessed to by ES-Basil) contains no Redemption themes, nor are they present even in the Byz-Basil amplification of this section. However, ATA and LJC, by contrast, already contain the theme of Redemption as well as Creation in the Preface, albeit in concise form (AB33-38). An awareness of this (coupled with the knowledge that such material occurs in the Anamnesis) *may* (along with sheer conservatism) have influenced the Redactors of ATA and LJC against copying Sy-Jas and Byz-Basil at this point.

Certainly the Redactor of the parent form behind ATA and LJC clearly was not interested in inserting a great deal of Redemption material at this point. What he *did* need, however, was a link to enable him to make the transition from the Sanctus to the Institution Narrative. John 3.16 conveniently provided a summary of God's saving provision (for which he could rightly be praised as 'Holy'), together with a mention of the Son of God who was to be the subject of the next section, the Institution Narrative. The section in ATA and LJC has all the signs of being a deliberate link, rather than part of an ancient core. We shall return to a discussion of the significance of this later.

---

[1] *Investigation* 59-76.

Looking at the text in detail, it will be observed that Byz-Basil and LJC share a common introduction (C1-3). As Engberding implies[1] this is likely to have come into Byz-Basil from an independent source (it is not found in the other Basiline versions) and from there to have made its way into LJC.

It is difficult to know whether the Trinitarian ascription which ATA and LJC share is not itself a secondary amplification of the *agios* of line C4. If it is, it must be of relatively early date. This raises the intriguing question as to whether or not ATA might not have influenced the Syrian tradition at this point. Certainly, the equivalent section of Sy-Jas could just as easily be an amplification of the ATA form as an independent development.

In conclusion it may be said that this section does appear to show a modest degree of influence on LJC by Byz-Basil, but it demonstrates more clearly a preference by the Redactors for their original source and pattern.

1D INSTITUTION NARRATIVE
Here, as both Engberding and Wagner are at pains to point out, a significant divergence between ATA and LJC begins to be apparent. Up until this point ATA had tended to possess the shorter text, from now on it frequently exceeds LJC in length and content. Furthermore, again as both Engberding and Wagner confirm, the similarities between ATA and Sy-Jas increase, to the point of identity in places.

Both these points are illustrated clearly in the Institution Narrative. Not only is the text of ATA visibly longer than that of LJC, but, as Table D shows, it is almost verbally identical, with the exception of a few phrases in Sy-Jas not found in ATA. Further, as Wagner points out[2] where there are agreements between ATA and LJC, these tend to be standard West Syrian forms and make the discovery of an ancestral version all the more difficult.

ATA's only significant points of departure from the text of Sy-Jas are the opening formula which it shares with LJC (and which is presumably therefore derived from the common original) (D4-5) and the omission of Sy-Jas' opening formula (D8).

LJC, on the other hand, shows signs of having resisted any attempt to assimilate it to the Byz-Basil form. It lacks a number of characteristically Basiline phrases (D1-3, 12-13, 37) as well as the reworked version of 1 Corinthians 11. It would seem difficult, therefore, to disagree with Engberding's conclusion that LJC preserves with little change the form of the Institutiuon Narrative found in the common ancestor which it shares with ATA.[3]

1E ANAMNESIS
With the Anamnesis verbal correlation between ATA and LJC becomes increasingly harder to trace and it is necessary to proceed one step at a time.

The Anamnesis in ATA is addressed to God the Son, and not to the Father. This is a standard Syrian practice and does not appear to affect substantially the content of the prayer.

---

[1] Zwolf, p.239.
[2] Ursprung, p.48.
[3] Zwolf, p.242.

Both ATA and LJC begin with a remembrance of Christ's saving command (E1-2) and to all that was done for us. This phrase occurs neither in Sy-Jas nor Byz-Basil and must therefore be reckoned part of the parent form. Both then have a list of various salvific events—cross, resurrection, ascension, session and second coming. Engberding appears to assume that these were part of the underlying original and comments on the lack of adjectives[1] It has been claimed that there is no trace of an Anamnesis in the works of St John Chrysostom, but Wagner is able to point to an impressive number of sequences of such events in the saint's sermons.[2] Even so, it should not be assumed uncritically that such a list formed part of the original text. The equivalent lists in Sy-Jas and Byz-Basil are almost identical (indeed, the present author has argued that they are versions of the same text[3] with the exception of a few relatively modest variations which could have taken place at a later stage of development. It will be demonstrated below that the second half of the Anamnesis could have been borrowed wholesale by both ATA and LJC; there is no reason why this list should not have been borrowed with it.

After the list of salvific events comes the oblation. In LJC this is identical with that of Byz-Basil (E21-22). The significance of this lies in the fact that the Byz-Basil form is not primitive, but is a remodelling of a simpler statement of offering which has survived in E-Basil. There are good reasons for dating this remodelling to about the year 370, which means it cannot have formed part of the LJC text before this date.

The text of ATA is very close to that of Sy-Jas with one extra-ordinary difference: whereas Sy-Jas contains *two* statements of offering (E22-25 and 43), ATA contains none at all. I have argued elsewhere that the two offerings in Sy-Jas are perhaps the result of the conflation of the old Jerusalemite anaphora with that of an E-Basil type.[4] Given that ATA is so close to Sy-Jas at this point, the omission of *both* of them is extremely intriguing. A partial parallel is provided by Sy-Basil which has a long embolism at this point (some of it identical with the ATA/Sy-Jas material here) which appears to have squeezed out any statement of offering. Sy-Basil, however, only had one oblation to miss out, as it were, ATA, if following Sy-Jas, has missed out two. Echoes of the second may be discerned in the *'pro omnibus et propter omnia'* (E44) where ATA is close to Sy-Basil. But the lack of any trace of Sy-Jas' E22-25 is remarkable. The exact link-up of the ATA text before and after these lines, makes it difficult to escape the impression that the offering statement was deliberately excised by the Redactor of ATA. Can it be that he was deliberately trying to create an oblationless anaphora? The idea would seem almost incredible were it not for the fact that the divergence of the ATA and LJC texts here poses the question: 'What was the form of the oblation in the common original?' No trace of it appears to survive in either

---

[1] Zwolf, p.243.
[2] Ursprung, p.110.
[3] *Investigation*, 207ff.
[4] *ibid.*

anaphora. Could it be that the very fact that ATA and LJC have to look independently elsewhere for material at this point, indicates that their parent form had
no equivalent section? Thus it might just be that the Redactor of ATA, while prepared to embellish his anaphora from Syrian sources, was not prepared to abandon what he may have felt to be an important feature of his ancient prayer,
namely the lack of any oblation. Neither Engberding nor Wagner address the
problem: we can only speculate.[1]

1F EPICLESIS

After such wide divergence in the preceding section it is all the more remarkable
to find ATA and LJC reverting to a substantial measure of agreement in the
Epiclesis.[2] ATA lacks most of the Sy-Jas embellishments (F21-31, 35-37, 46-49,
55-56, 89-95), while LJC lacks much of the Byz-Basil material, including some of
its characteristic phrases (e.g. *eudokia tes ses agathotetos* (F15)). It is true that LJC
shows some signs of being influenced by Byz-Basil (eg *eph'emas, eis koinonian tes
agiou sou pneumatos* (F19, 65), but it also asserts its independence by having
katapempson instead of *elthein* (F16), and, retaining forgiveness of sins as one of
the fruits of communion (F61)).

The main differences between ATA and LJC are the phrase 'falling on our
faces' (F101) in the former, and a more explicit statement of the transforming
work of the Holy Spirit on the elements in the latter. In the second part of the
Epiclesis (F57-71) the points of contact between the two continue, though LJC
stops short and does not have the paragraph F78-87 of ATA.

This paragraph merits further examination. It has all the appearance of a summing up or concluding petition, asking for preservation, grace to minister before
God, and enjoyment of the heavenly mysteries, ending with the formula 'now
and to the ages of ages'. Parallels can be discerned with Ap Trad, Theodore of
Mopsuestia[3]; the Deir Balyzeh Papyrus[4] where a summing up petition concludes
the prayer; and even St Mark itself[5]

The content, and concluding formula, together with the unconnected way in
which the Intercessions follow, make it difficult to escape the conclusion that we
have here the original ending of the Epiclesis, and in all probability, of the
original prayer itself. This has been lost in LJC in the process of its assimilation to
Byz-Basil, but retained in ATA where the Redactor has prefered it to the
equivalent section F88-95 (itself an ancient ending?) in Sy-Jas. We shall return to
the implications of this in our discussion below.

---

[1] The parallels with Sy-Basil prompt the question whether it is this anaphora and not Sy-
Jas that the Redactor of ATA was following. In fact examination of the texts rules this
out—the content and structure of Sy-Basil are further removed from ATA than is Sy-Jas.
[2] Engberding missed this completely, concluding, 'the correlations are diminishing', Zwolf
p.243).
[3] He prays that the grace of the Holy Spirit may come upon all gathered together, that they
may be united as into one body by partaking of the body of our Lord . . and that they
may be one in concord, peace and well-doing.' PEER p.86).
[4] PEER p.45.
[5] PEER p.54.

1G INTERCESSIONS

The Intercessions are usually a complex and fluid section of ancient anaphoras, reflecting as they do changing situations after the rest of the prayer has become fixed in form. For the purposes of the present paper a detailed textual comparison of the various forms is unnecessary: it will suffice merely to look at the sequences of the petitions in the anaphoras.[1]

From Table G it is clear that in Sy-Jas and ATA the basic petition sequence (A, B, C, etc.) is the same. There are some deviations—eg J is displaced in Sy-Jas, and N in ATA—but despite these and the interpolation of various other petitions, the sequences are close enough to have derived from a common pattern.

LJC and Byz-Basil also exhibit similarities. Both begin with a common block relating to the departed before going on to a rather more random sequence covering the needs of the living. Once again, the sequence is close enough to be accounted for by the derivation of one from the other or of both from a common source.

However, there is very little correlation between the basic sequence shared by Sy-Jas and ATA on the one hand, and that shared by LJC and Byz-Basil on the other. It looks very much as though the Redactors of ATA and LJC took their Intercessions from independent sources—the same sources from which they had already taken material earlier in the anaphora.

This is confirmed by the fact that the dead/living sequence, which is a reversal of the primitive order, can be demonstrated to have been made in the Basiline anaphora almost certainly in response to a cue in the primitive Basiline Epiclesis.[2] No such starting point exists in LJC, which must have derived its Intercession sequence entire from elsewhere.

All this strongly confirms the secondary nature of the Intercessions in both anaphoras and increases the likelihood that the Epiclesis ending in ATA (F78-87) is the ancient ending of the prayer.

1H DOXOLOGY

There is little that need be said about the Doxologies of the four anaphoras. As might be expected, that of ATA is virtually identical with Sy-Jas, and that of LJC with that of Byz-Basil. Each has presumably been incorporated along with the preceding Intercessions.

CONCLUSIONS

1) Our investigation has shown that the highest levels of agreement between ATA and LJC are to be found in:

    Preface
    Pre-Sanctus
    Post-Sanctus
    Institution Narrative
    Epiclesis

---

[1] For ease of cross-reference the system of nomenclature of petitions is a slightly modified version of that used in *Investigation* 250-338. For the purposes of this Study it is the Intercessions labelled 'A', 'B' etc. (in bold capitals) which are of particular interest. See also footnote 1 on page 32.

[2] *Investigation* 287-295.

2) There is least agreement in content and structure in the Anamnesis/ Oblation and in the Intercessions.

3) Throughout the anaphora ATA shows signs of having picked up Sy-Jas phrases and features, LJC those of Byz-Basil. In the Anamnesis/Oblation, Intercessions and at other points of substantial verbal disagreement, ATA follows closely the text of Sy-Jas, and LJC that of Byz-Basil. We are therefore left with the possibility that the common original behind ATA and LJC lacked these sections.

4) The present writer has already shown that in the late fourth century anaphoras could be 'improved' by incorporating into them sections from elsewhere which had come to be felt to be desirable or necessary in a 'complete' prayer.[1] If the form ancestral to ATA and LJC did indeed lack an Anamnesis/ Oblation and Intercessions (and about the latter there can hardly be any doubt) then it looks very much as though two independent Redactors sought to improve it by importing these sections from already existing prayers that were deemed to be good models in this respect. The result can be represented diagrammatically:

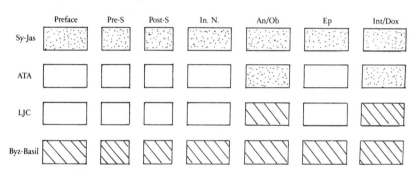

We can now turn to examine the text of AC in the light of these findings.

---

[1] *Investigation* passim.

Part 2

THE ANAPHORA OF APOSTOLIC CONSTITUTIONS BOOK VIII IN RELATION TO ATA AND LJ

Much work still remains to be done on the development of the long and complex anaphora of AC. Various sources of influence and material have been identified[1], but little progress has been made in identifying an original source. The form of the prayer is characteristically West Syrian and its intercessions suggest a large city, namely Antioch itself. This being the case, it seems reasonable to compare it with LJC and ATA, both of which are also associated with Antioch.

Such a comparison is complicated by two factors:

a) the sheer length of AC. This has been solved here by simply omitting from the Tables large blocks of material which appear to bear no significant relation to any part of the texts of LJC.

b) the fact that AC shows signs of having *two* Pre-Sanctuses, two Anamneses (and see parallel columns:, AB56-58 and E1-20). This strengthens the likelihood of the text having derived from two or more sources, but makes presentation somewhat difficult. As can be seen from the Tables, where AC possesses two similar sections, both are shown in parallel with the equivalent sections in the other liturgies. This involves some relocation of material, such passages being indicated by a line down the left hand side.

The following discussion takes for granted many of the points raised in the first section of this paper, which are therefore not repeated here.

2A PREFACE

AC begins with an expanded form of the *Axion kai dikaion* which we have already noted as being a likely part of the common original of ATA and LJC. The phrase is of course a fairly widespread one, but its presence should not be underestimated.

AC is now remarkable for the relative paucity of its praise-verbs, which is all the more significant in view of the Redactor's desire to pile up words at other points (e.g. the attributes of God AB18). The only verb in fact is *anumnein* which finds an eqquivalent in LJC. Significantly there is no *eucharistein*, which supports its absence in ATA, as discussed above. The most reasonable explanation for the lack of praise verbs would seem to be that the Redactor was working from a text with few such verbs and saw no need to augment at this point.

The AC phrase *ton ontos onta theon* is also found in Byz-Basil and has an echo in the *aei on osautos on* of LJC. As ATA lacks the phrase it is difficult to know what to make of the relationship of LJC and AC here. It is just possible that they preserve memories of a phrase in the original.

---

[1] See, for example, the works cited in PEER.

AC now embarks on a list of attributes of God the Creator, which have caused the removal of the mention of the Son and the Holy Spirit here (AB18), but returns to a point of contact with ATA and LJC with *o ta panta ek tou me ontos eis to einai paragagon* (AB32-33). The object of the phrase is 'us' in ATA and LJC, but 'all things' in AC, which is not surprising as the Redactor of AC clearly intends to survey the creation of the natural world at length before addressing the creation of man, whereas ATA and LJC are embarking directly on the Divine Economy towards the fallen human race. AC has some material equivalent to this section, but much further on in the Preface.

2B PRE-SANCTUS

ATA and LJC conclude their brief Prefaces with a summing up thanksgiving to the Trinity (AB39) before proceeding to the Cherubim and Seraphim and the heavenly praises.

AC also looks as though it is going to proceed directly to a Sanctus, but instead reverts to a lengthy description of Creation, Fall and Salvation History as far as Joshua before continuing with a full listing of heavenly beings and the congregational Sanctus. Both its 'false' and 'true' Pre-Sanctus texts are shown side by side on Table AB. A number of points deserve comment.

a) When the Redactor of AC does get round to his true Pre-Sanctus, he feels the need to introduce it with a summing up phrase: *huper apanton soi he doxa, despota pantokrator.* Interestingly, this is precisely what we have seen ATA and LJC do (and the AC text is placed in parallel to them, AB39). This could well reflect a link which the Redactor of AC felt important to express and which he retained, despite his extensive reworking of the prayer at this point.

b) the 'false' Pre-Sanctus in AC is remarkably brief, as are those of ATA and LJC. The Cherubim and Seraphim are mentioned without any further description, which is even briefer than ATA and LJC. The following block (AB72-75) has all the appearance of a later insertion, departing as it does from the 'standard' sequence, with the interesting exception of the archangels and angels which occur in this position also in the true Pre-Sanctus (AB74) in wording similar to that found in LJC (AB59). This raises the possibility that the parent text may have listed Cherubim, Seraphim, archangels and angels (note the reversal of the usual order in the case of the latter pair), and the influence of Sy-Jas and Byz-Basil may have prompted the transference of the archangels and angels in the case of ATA and LJC, while the two Pre-Sanctuses of AC preserve the original sequence.

c) With the exception of the archangels just discussed, the true Pre-Sanctus of AC looks very much as though it is simply following what was becoming a standard format, witnessed to by Sy-Jas and Byz-Basil. It could well be a wholesale borrowing from another source, slightly modified in the light of some of the Redactor's traditional usages.

PREFACE

	Sy-Jas	ATA	LJC
1			
2			
3	vere dignum et iustum	dignum et iustum est	αξιον και δικαιον
4	et decens et debitum		
5			
6		nos te adorare	
7	nos te glorificare	et te glorificare	
8	tibi benedicere		
9	te laudare		σε υμνειν
10	te adorare		
11	tibi gratias agere		σοι ευχαριστειν
12			σε προσκυνειν
13			εν παντι τοπω της σης δεσποτειας σου
14		qui vere es Deus	συ γαρ ει θεος
15			ανεκφραστος απερινοητας αορατος
16			ακαταλητος
17			αει ων ωσαυτως ων
18			
19		et unigenitum filium tuum	συ και ο μονογενης σου υιος
20		et spiritum sanctum	και το πνευμα σου το αγιον
21			
22			
23			
24			
25			
26			
27			
28			
29			
30			
31	factori totius creationis		
32	visibilis sane et invisibilis		
33		tu enim ex eo quod non est ad hoc ut	συ εκ του μη οντος εις το ειναι
34		adduxisti (nos	ημας παρηγαγες
35		et quando lapsi eramus tunc iterum re-	και παραπεσοντας ανεστησας παλιν
36		vocasti nos et non destiti operari	και ουκ απεστης παντα ποιων
37		donec caelum ascendere facies	εως ημας εις τον ουρανον ανηγαγες
38		et regnum futurum dares nobis	και την βασιλειαν εχαριοω την μελλουσαν
39		propter haec omnia gratias agimus tibi	υπερ τουτων απαντων ευχαριστουμεν σοι
40		et unigenito filio tuo	και τω μονογενει σου υιω
41		et spiritui sancto	και τω πνευματι σου τω αγιω
42			
43			υπερ παντων ων ισμεν και ων ουκ ισμεν
44			των φανερων και αφανων ευεργεσιων σου
45			των εις ημας γεγενημενων
46			ευχαριστουμεν σοι και υπερ της λειτουργιας
47			ταυτης ην εκ των χειρων ημων δεξασθαι
48			καταξιωσον
49			
50			
51			
52	quem glorificant		
53	caeli caelorum et omnes virtutes eorum		
54	sol et luna et omnis chorus stellarum		
55	terra maria omnique quod in eis		
56	Ierusalem caelestis ecclesia primo-		
57	genitorum qui scripto sunt in caelo		
58		ante te enim stant in circuitu	καιτοι σοι παρεστηκεισαν
59	angeli archangeli		χιλιαδεσς αρχαγγελων και μυριαδεσ|αγγελων
60	principatus potestates		
61	throni dominationes		
62	virtutes quae supra mundum		
63	exercitus caelestes		
64	cherubim multos occulos	cherubim quattuor facies (habentes)	τα χερουβειμ
65			
66	et seraphim	et seraphim	και τα σεραφειμ
67	sex alas (habentes)	sex alas (habentes)	εξαπτερυγα πολυομματε
68	qui duabus quidem alis tegunt facies suas		μεταρσια πτερωτα
69	duabus vero pedes duabus volitant		
70			
71	alter ad alterum		
72			
73			
74			
75			
76		laudem majestatis	
77	oribus non quiescentibus	oribus non silentibus	
78	et theologia non conticescenti	et vocibus non tacentibus	
79	hymnum triumphalem magnificentia gloriae		τον επινικιον υμνον
80	voce clara		
81	glorificantes vociferantes	glorificantes vociferantes	αδοντα
82	clamantes et dicentes	et clamantes et dicentes	
83			
84			
85			
86			
87			
88			

18 'The Missing Oblation': The Contents of the Early Antiochene Anaphora

Preface and Pre-Sanctus

	Byz-Basil	AC
1	ο ων δεσποτα κυριε θεε πατερ	
2	παντοκρατορ προσκυνητε	
3	αξιον ως αληθως και δικαιον	αξιον ως αληθως και δικαιον
4	και πρεπον	
5	τη μεγαλοπρεπεια της αγιωσυνης σου	
6		
7	σε αινειν	
8		
9	σε υμνειν σε ευλογειν	ανυμνειν σε
10	σε προσκυνειν	
11	σοι ευχαριστειν	
12	σε δοξαζειν	
13		
14	τον μονον οντως οντα θεον	τον οντως οντα θεον
15		
16		
17		
18		[List of epithets of God]
19		
20		
21	σοι προσφερειν	
22	εν καρδια συντετριμμενη και πνευματι	
23	ταπεινωσεως την λογικεν ταυτεν λατρειαν	
24	ημων. οτι συ ει ο χαρισαμενος ημιν την	
25	επιγνωσιν της σης αληθειας και τις	
26	ικανος λαλησαι τας δυναστειας σου ακουσ-	
27	τας ποιησαι πασας τας αινεσεις σου η	
28	διηγησασθαι παντα τα θαυματα σου εν παν	
29	-τι καιρω	
30	δεσποτα δεσποτα των απαντων	
31	κυριε ουρανου και γη και πασης κτισεως	
32	ορωμενης τε και ουκ ορωμενης	
33		ο τα παντα εκ του μη οντος εις το ειναι
34		παραγαγων
35		
36		
37		
38		
39		υπερ απαντων σοι η δοξα δεσποτα παντοκρατορ
40		δια του μονογενους σου υιου
41		αυτον δε προ παντων...
42		[list of Christological titles]
43		
44		
45		
46		
47		
48		
49	ο καθημενος επι θρονου δοξης...	
50	[epithets of the Trinity]	
51		ο δι αυτου προ παντων ποιησας
52	σε γαρ αινουσιν	
53		
54		
55		
56		
57		
58		σε προσκυνουμεν
59	αγγελοι αρχαγγελοι	αναριθμοι στρατιαι αγγελων αρχαγγελων
60		
61	θρονοι κυριοτητες	θρονων κυριοτητων
62	εξουσιαι δυναμεις	αχρων
63		εξουσιων δυναμεων
64	και τα πολυομματα χερουβειμ	τα χερουβιμ στρατιων αιωνιων
65	σοι παρισταντα κυκλω	
66	τα σεραφειμ	και τα σεραφειμ τα χερουβιμ
67	εξ πτερυγες τω ενι και εξ πτερυγες τω ενι	
68	και ταις μεν δυσι κατακαλυπτουσιν τα	και τα εξαπτερυγα σεραφιμ
69	προσωπα εαυτων και ταις δυσιν τους ποδας	ταις μεν δυσιν κατακαλυπτοντα τους
70	και ταις δυσι πετομενα	ποδας ταις δυσι τας κεφαλας
71	κεκραγεν ετερον προς το ετερον	ταις δε δυσι πετομενα
72		αιωνιας τε και στρατιας και λεγοντα αμα χιλιαις χιλιασιν
73		δυναμεις τε και εξουσιας αρχαγγελων και μυριαις μυριασιν αγγελων
74		αρχας τε και θρονους
75		αρχαγγελους τε και αγγελους ακαταπαυστως και ασιγητως
76		
77	ακαταπαυστοις στομασιν	βοωσαις
78	ασιγητοις θεολογιαις	
79	τον επινικιον υμνον	και πας ο λαος αμα ειπατω
80		
81	αδοντα βοωντα	
82	κεκραγοτα και λεγοντα	
83		και μετα ταυτα παντα ποιησας
84		δι αυτου τον φαινομενον τουτον
85		κοσμον και παντα τα εν αυτω
86		[Recital of Creation, Fall and
87		Creation History to Joshua,
88		followed by pre-Sanctus material]

2C POST-SANCTUS

Like Byz-Basil and Sy-Jas, AC has a relatively long Post-Sanctus which moves, like theirs, from the Fall, via the Law and the Prophets, to the Incarnation and the earthly ministry of Christ. None of this is present in ATA or Jas, which is not altogether surprising since they have already given thanks for redemption in their Preface, and in view of the fact that the Christological Post-Sanctus is itself a late development.[1]

In contrast, ATA and LJC have a simple ascription of holiness to the Trinity (with an opening borrowed from Byz-Basil in LJC), followed by John 3:16 as an introduction to the Institution Narrative. The only part of this which AC shares is the opening phrase of the ascription (somewhat embellished), together with what looks like the remnant of the remainder of the trinitarian formula (C4-7). Instead of mentioning also the Holy Spirit, the Redactor has linked his Christological material directly to *hagios de kai o monogenes sou uiou.*

Table C

	Sy-Jas	ATA	LJC
1			μετα τουτων και ημεις των δυναμε
2			δεσποτα φιλανθρωπε
3			βοωμεν και λεγωμεν
4	sicut vere sanctus es	sanctus es tu et sanctissimus	αγοις ει και παναγιος
5	et rex saeculorum		
6	et dator omnis sactitatis		
7	sanctus et unigenitus filius tuus	et unigenitus filius tuus	και ο μονογενης σου Υιος
8	Dominus et Deus noster Jesus Christus		
9	sanctus vero et spiritus tuus sanctus	et spiritus tuus sanctus	και το πνευμα σου το αγιον
10	qui scrutatur omnia et profunda tua		
11	Deus et Pater		
12	sanctus enim es	sanctus es tu et sanctissimus	αγιος ει και παναγιος
13		et magnificentia gloria tua	και μεγαλοπρεπης η δοξα σου
14		qui ita dilexistis mundum	ως τον κοσμον σου ουτως ηγαπησας
15		ut filium tuum unigenitum	ωστε τον υιον σου τον μονογενη
16		dares pro illo	δουναι
17		ut omnes qui credunt in eum	ινα πας ο πιστευων εις αυτον
18		ne pereant sed habeant vitam aeternam	μη αποληται αλλ'εχη ζωην αιωνιον

[Long section on Economy of Salvation]

---

[1] See Fenwick, *Investigation* 59-76.

The material itself at first sight appears a fairly standard recital of the salvific events, but on more detailed examination contains at two places terminology reminiscent of ATA and LJC and evidence of a degree of reworking of the content:

a) At the end of the summary of Jesus' earthly ministry, and linking it to the account of his arrest, trial and crucifixion, are a couple of lines which contain an echo of ATA/LJC material (D4-7). The idea of Jesus' coming and *fulfilling all* things is common to all three texts and provides an interesting example of AC echoing an idea in the common inheritanace of ATA and LJC. It may therefore be a turn of phrase that the Redactor was unwilling to lose, despite his drastic reworking of this section.

b) AC concludes its account of the salvific events with what might be termed a 'false Anamnesis' (E1-6). The text of this will be discussed below.

Post-Sanctus

Byz-Basil

1 μετα τουτων των μακαριων δυναμεων
2 δεσποτα φιλανθρωπε και ημεις οι αμαρτωλοι
3 βοωμεν και λεγομεν
4 αγιος ει ως αληθως και παναγιος
5
6
7
8
9
10
11
12
13
14
15
16
17
18

AC

αγιος γαρ ει ως αληθως και παναγιος
υψιστος και υπερυψουμενος εις τους αιωνας

αγιος δε και ο μονογενης σου Υιος

[Long section on Economy of Salvation]   [Long section on Economy of Salvation]

2D INSTITUTION NARRATIVE

As has already been discussed, Table D4-7 shows embedded in the Post-Sanctus material of AC a phrase which bears some similarity to the formula with which ATA and LJC begin their Institution Narratives. This would point towards there being such a Narrative in the common source.

AC's own Narrative shows a number of words and phrases not shared with the other texts under review here, but in general looks to be an elaboration of a relatively unembellished text. There are, for example, remarkably few verbs de-

Table D

NARRATIVE OF INSTITUTION

	Sy-Jas	ATA	LJC
1			
2			
3			
4		qui cum venisset et totam oeconomian	ος ελθων και πασαν την υπερ υμων
5		quae pro nobis est adimplevisset	οικονομιαν πληρωσας
6			
7			
8	cum vero suscepturus esset		
9			
10			
11			
12			
13	mortem voluntariam		
14	pro nobis peccatoribus ille qui		
15	sine peccato		
16	nocte illa qua tradebatur	nocte illa qua traditus est	τη νυκτι η παρεδιδου εαυτον
17	pro vita et salute mundi		
18	accipiens panem	accepit panem	λαβων αρτον
19	super manus suas sanctas	in manus suas sanctas	εν ταις αγιαις αυτου
20	et immaculataset incontaminatas		και αχραντοις και αμωμητοις χερσιν
21	et ostendit tibi Dei et Patri	et postquam extendit ad caelum	
22	et gratias agens		ευχαριστησας
23	benedixit sanctificavit	benedixit sanctificavit	και ευλογησας
24	fregit	fregit	εκλασεν
25	dedit discipulis suis	et dedit discipulis suis	και εδωκεν τοις αγιοις αυτου μαθη
26	et apostolis dicens	apostolis dicens	και αποστολοις ειπων
27			
28	accipite manducate	accipite manducate	λαβετε φαγετε
29	ex eo vos omnes	ex eo vos omnes	
30	hoc meum est corpus	hoc est corpus meum	τουτ'εστιν το σωμα μου
31	quod pro vos	quod pro vos	το υπερ υμων
32	et pro multis	et pro multis	
33	frangitur et datur	frangitur et datur	
34	in remissionem peccatorum	in remmissionem (peccatorum)	
35	et in vitam aeternam	et in vitam aeternam	
36	similiter et calicem	similiter et calicem	ομοιως και το ποτεριον
37			
38	postquam cenaverunt	postquam cenaverunt	μετα το δειπνησαι
39	miscens vino et aqua	miscens e vino et aqua	
40	gratias egit	gratias egit	
41	benedixit sanctificavit	benedixit sanctificavit	
42		et postquam gustavit de illis	
43	dedit iisdem discipulis et apostolis	dedit discipulis suis apostolis	
44			
45	dicens	dicens	λεγων
46	accipite bibite ex eo omnes vos	accipite bibite ex eo vos omnes	πιετε εξ αυτου παντες
47	hic meus est sanguis	hic est sanguis	τουτ'εστιν το αιμα μου
48	testamenti novi	testamenti novi	το της καινης διαθηκης
49	qui pro vobis et pro multis	qui pro vobis et pro multis	το υπερ υμων και πολλων
50	effunditur et datur	effunditur et datur	εκχυνομενον
51	in remissionem peccatorum	in remissionem peccatorum	εις αφεσιν αμαρτιων
52	et in vitam aeternam. amen	et in vitam aeternam	
53	hoc facite in commemorationem meam	hoc facite in commemorationem meam	
54	quotiescumque enim manducabitis	quotiescumque enim manducabitis	
55	panem hunc et calicem hunc bibetis	panem hunc et calicem hunc bibetis	
56	mortem meam annuntiabitis	mortem meam annuntiabitis	
57		et resurrectionem meam confitebimini	
58	donec veniam	donec veniam	
59	People: Mortem tuam Domine noster...	People: mortem tuam Domine....	

scribing Jesus' actions. Similarly, the apostles are not qualified with various adjectives, and, indeed, at the Cup words, are merely *autous*.

At some points AC lacks material shared by ATA and LJC (D22-23, 48), while at others (for example, the use of *legon* instead of the Basiline *eipon* D45) there are affinities with the ATA/LJC text. Nevertheless the number of small differences make it difficult to claim that here is simply the ATA/LJC Narrative slightly altered. It *could* be, but it would not be impossible to claim that the entire Narrative was taken from some other source.

Narrative of Institution

	Byz-Basil	AC
1	κατελιπε δε ημιν υπομνηματα του	
2	σωτηριου αυτου παθους ταυτα α	
3	προτεθεικαμεν κατα της αυτου εντολα	
4		το θελημα σου
5		επληρωσεν
6		το εργον ο εδωκας αυτω ετελειωσεν
7		και ταυτα παντα κατορθωσας
8	μελλων γαρ εξιεναι	χερσιν ανομων κατασχεθεις...
9		[Account of Passion, Resurrection and
10		Ascension, followed by 'false
11		Anamnesis' E1-6]
12	επι τον εκουσιον και αοιδιμον και	
13	ζωοποιον αυτου θανατον	
14		
15		
16	εν τη νυκτι η παρεδιδου εαυτον	εν η γαρ νυκτι παρεδιδετο
17	υπερ της του κοσμου ζωης	
18	λαβων αρτον	λαβων αρτον
19	επι των αγιων αυτου	ταις αγιαις
20	και αχραντων χειρων	και αμμοις αυτου χερσιν
21	και αναδειξας σοι τω θεω και πατρι	και αναβλεψας προς σε τον θεον αυτου και πατερα
22	ευχαριστησας	
23	ευλογησας αγιασας	
24	κλασας	και κλασας
25	εδωκεν τοις αγιοις αυτου μαθηταις	εδωκεν τοις μαθηταις
26	και αποστολοις ειπων	ειπων
27		τουτο το μυστηριον μου της καινης διαθηκης
28	λαβετε φαγετε	λαβετε εξ αυτου φαγετε
29		
30	τουτο μου εστιν το σωμα	τουτο εστι το σωμα μου
31	το υπερ υμων	
32		το περι πολλων
33	κλωμενον	θρυπτομενον
34	εις αφεσιν αμαρτιων	εις αφεσιν αμαρτιων
35		
36	ομοιως και το ποτεριον	ωσαυτως και το ποτεριον
37	εκ του γεννηματος της αμπελου λαβων	
38		
39	κερασας	κερασας εξ οινου και υδατος
40	ευχαριστησας	
41	ευλογησας αγιασας	και αγιασας
42		
43	εδωκεν τοις αγιοις αυτου μαθηταις	εδωκεν αυτοις
44	και αποστολοις	
45	ειπων	λεγων
46	πιετε εξ αυτου παντες	πιετε εξ αυτου παντες
47	τουτο μου εστιν το αιμα	τουτο εστι το αιμα μου
48		
49	το υπερ υμων και πολλων	το περι πολλων
50	εκχυνομενον	εκχυνομενον
51	εις αφεσιν αμαρτιων	εις αφεσιν αμαρτιων
52		
53	τουτο ποιειτε εις την εμυν αναμνησιν	τουτο ποιειτε εις την εμην αναμνησιν
54	οσακις γαρ αν εσθιητε τον αρτον τουτον	οσακις γαρ αν εσθιητε τον αρτον τουτον
55	και το ποτηριον τουτον πινητε	και πινητε το ποτεριον τουτο
56	τον εμον θανατον καταγγελλετε	τον θανατον τον εμον καταγγελλετε
57	και εμην αναστασιν ομολογειτε	
58	αχρις αν ελθω	
59		

2E ANAMNESIS

ATA and LJC begin their Anamnesis with a common formula 'We therefore, remembering his saving command and all that was done for us' (E1-6). There is no hint of this in AC's 'true' Anamnesis which simply launches into a list of the passion, death, resurrection, etc. There are, however, definite echoes in the so-called 'false' Anamnesis (set out at E1-6 for ease of comparison) to which attention was drawn above in the Post-Sanctus material. Here the two ideas of 'what he endured for us' and 'his saving command', despite the reversed order and the use of *diataxis* instead of *entole*, seem to preserve the same ideas juxtaposed.

Indeed the likelihood is strengthened when the relation of the idea of the 'saving command' to the Institution Narrative is examined further. In ATA and LJC the words appear to refer back to the command to eat and drink in remembrance of Christ in the preceding Narrative. In the 'false' Anamnesis of ATA, the concept is used to *introduce* the Narrative which follows. Furthermore, the concept of the command was clearly an important one to the Redactor of AC, for he has introduced it again in his 'true' Anamnesis (E24). This short section, it is widely recognized, has been taken from the Apostolic Tradition, which makes the Redactor's determination to insert the concept of the command into an externally-derived section of text all the more remarkable. It was clearly an understanding of the Eucharist that he was not willing to abandon, presumably because it formed an important link in his original text, as witnessed to by ATA and LJC.

Highly significant, too, is the presence of the Hippolytan-derived oblation. As has already been noted in Part 1, there is no trace of a common oblation in ATA and LJC which have had to derive such material independently from other anaphoras. If AC is also derived from the same parent form, then the fact that it too has had to seek its oblation from elsewhere would seem to greatly strengthen the likelihood that the original contained no oblation.

Is it however possible that AC in fact preserves the original form in the 'false' Anamnesis (E1-6)?

'Remembering therefore what he endured for us, we give you thanks, almighty God, not as we ought but as we are able, and we fulfill his command.'

Is *we give you thanks* the ancient heart of the Antiochene Anamnesis, and indeed of its anaphora? Brightman was unable to find evidence of a 'full' Anamnesis or of an Oblation in the writings of John Chrysostom[1] and, although Wagner found some material which resembled the traditional list, he too was unable to produce unequivocal evidence of an oblation.[2] There is certainly an inner logic to such a progression: Having hymned God for his work of salvation, praised him in the Sanctus, remembered the sending of his only Son and the Son's command to eat and drink in remembrance of him, we fulfill that command and give thanks.

---

[1] LEW, p.35.
[2] *op. cit.*

Such a sequence could still be followed appropriately by an Epiclesis, as will be discussed below.

Certainly the primacy of thanksgiving would accord well with the emphasis shown in AB39, where 'for all these things we give you thanks' sums up the Preface (and, indeed, may be the climax of the ancient 'mini-anaphora'). If it be accepted that the 'false' Anamnesis of AC is indeed the same material as the Anamnesis introductions of ATA and LJC, then the likelihood of its being the original form in the parent text, would seem to be very strong indeed.

	Sy-Jas	ATA	LJC
1	memores igitur Domine	dum igitur memores sumus Domine	μεμνημενοι τοινυν
2		praecepti salutaris	της σωτηριου ταυτης εντολης
3			
4			
5		et totius oeconomiae tua	και παντων
6		qua pro nobis facta est	το υπερ ημων γεγενημενον
7	mortis tuae		
8		crucis	του σταυρου
9			
10			του ταφου
11	et resurrectionis tuae terta die a mortis	resurrectionis tertia die a mortis	της τριημερου αναστασεως
12	et ascensionis tuae in caelum	et ascensionis in caelum	της εις ουρανουος αναβασεως
13	et sessionis tuae ad dexteram	et sessionis ad dexteram	της εκ δεξιων καθεδρας
14	Dei et Patris	majestatis Patris	
15	et adventus tui secundi	et adventus tui secundi	της δευτερας και ενδοξου παλιν
16	tremendi et gloriosi	gloriosi	παρουσιας
17	quo iudicaturus es orbem in iustitia	in quo futurus es cum gloria iudicare	
18		vivos et mortos	
19	cum retributurus es unicuique	et retribuere omnibus hominibus	
20	secundum opera eius	secunda opera eorum	
21			τα σα εκ των σων
22	offerimus tibi		σοι προσφεροντες
23			
24			
25	hoc sacrificium tremendum et incruendum		
26			
27			
28			
29	ne secundum peccata nostra facias nobis		
30	Domine neque secundum iniquitates		
31	nostras retribuas nobis		
32	sed secundum mansuetudinem et phil-	cum philanthropia	
33	anthropiam tuam		
34	dele peccata nostra		
35	obsecrantium te populus enim tuus	namque supplicat tibi ecclesia t	
36	et heridatas tua obsecrat te	et grex tuus	
37	et per te et tecum Patrem	et per te ac tecum Patri tuo	
38	dicens	dicens	
39		Misereri mei	
40	People: miserere nostri.....	People: miserere nostri	
41	Priest: et nos quoque tibi gratias	Priest: nos quoque Domine gratias agentes	
42	agentes et confitemur tibi	confitemur tibi	
43	ex tuo tibi offerimus tibi		
44	in omnibus et propter omnia	pro omnibus et propter omnia	κατα παντα και δια παντα
45	People: te laudamus...	People: te laudamus tibi benedicimus tibi	People: σε υμνουμεν σε ευλογουμεν
46		gratias agimus Domine	ευχαριστουμεν κυριε
47		et rogamus te Deus noster	και δεομεθα σου ο θεος ημων
48		propitius esto o bone et miserere nostri	

Anamnesis

Byz-Basil	AC	
1 μεμνημενοι ουν δεσποτα και ημεις	μεμνημενοι ουν	μεμνημενοι τοινυν
2 ων δι'ημας υπεμειναν		
3	ευχαριστουμεν σοι θεε παντοκρατορ	
4	ουχ οσον οφειλομεν αλλ'οσον δυναμεθα	
5		
6	και την διαταξιν πληρουμεν	
7 των σωτηριων αυτου παθηματων		του παθους αυτου
8 του ζωοποιου σταυρου		και του θανατου
9		
10 της τριημερου ταφης		και της εκ νεκρων αναστασεως
11 της εκ νεκρων αναστασεως		και της εις ουρανους επανοδου
12 της εις ουρανους ανοδου		
13 της εκ δεξιων σου		
14 του θεου και πατρος καθεδρας		και της μελλουσης αυτου δευτερας
15 και της ενδοξου και φοβερας δευτερας		παπουσιας
16 αυτου παρουσιας		εν η ερχεται μετα δοξης και δυναμεως
17		κριναι ζωντας και νεκρους
18		και αποδουναι εκαστω
19		κατα τα εργα αυτου
20		
21 τα σα εκ των σων		προσφερομεν σοι
22 σοι προσφεροντες		τω βασιλει και θεω
23		κατα την αυτου διαταξιν
24		τον αρτον τουτον και το ποτηριον τουτο
25		ευχαριστουντες σοι δι'αυτου εφ'οις
26		καταξιωσας ημας εστανοι ενωπιον σου
27		και ιερατευειν σοι
28		
29		
30		
31		
32		
33		
34		
35		
36		
37		
38		
39		
40		
41		
42		
43		
44 κατα παντα και δια παντα		
45 People: σε υμνουμεν σε ευλογουμεν σοι		
46 ευχαριστουμεν κυριε		
47 και δεομεθα σου ο θεος ημων		
48		

2F EPICLESIS

Once the influence of Sy-Jas and Byz-Basil on ATA and LJC respectively has been taken into account, the common material in the Epiclesis is quite brief: simply a request for God to send the Holy Spirit on the gifts set forth and to make (or show) the bread and wine the Body and Blood of his Christ so that they might be to the recipients for forgivness of sins and for boldness. Significantly, most of this core can be paralleled in AC. Several features suggest that all three Epicleses may be versions of a single original:

a) AC agrees with ATA and LJC in having *katapempto* as its main verb.

b) Neither ATA nor AC request the sending of the Holy Spirit on the worshippers, but only on the gifts. LJC appears to have been assimilated to Byz-Basil here, while ATA has resisted the influence of Sy-Jas. It looks as though ATA and AC thus preserve a single Epiclesis in contrast to the double Epiclesis of the Basiline tradition.

c) The sequence verb-Spirit-gifts is found in all three, ATA having resisted Sy-Jas's reversal of the last two.

d) AC's use of the word *thusia* at this point need cause no problems. The Redactor has already used the traditional phrase in what is presumably his own opening composition (F2), and therefore needed another word in the main petition.

Table F

	Sy-Jas	ATA	LJC
1			
2			
3			
4			
5			ετι προσφερομεν σοι την λογικεν ταυτη
6			και αναιμακτον λατρειαν
7	miserere nostri Deus Pater et Pantocrator		
8		deinde vero petimus a te	και παρακαλουμεν
9		Domine omnipotens et Deus virtutum sanct-	
10		arum super facies nostras cadentes ante te	
11			και δεομεθα
12			
13			και ικτευομεν
14			
15			
16	et mitte	ut mittas	καταπεμψον
17		spiritum sanctum	το πνευμα σου το αγιον
18	super nos		εφ' ημας
19	et super oblationes has propositas	super oblationes has quae propositae sunt	και επι τα προκειμενα δωρα ταυτα
20			
21	spiritum tuum sanctum		
22	Dominum et vivificantem consedentem tibi		
23	Deo Patri et Filio et conregnantem et		
24	consubstantialem et coaeternum		
25	qui locutus est in lege et prophetis		
26	et in testamento tuo novo		
27	qui descendit in similitudine columbae		
28	super Dominum nostrum Iesum Christum in		
29	Iordane flumine		
30	qui descendit super apostolos tuos in		
31	similitudine linguarum ignearum		
32	ut illabens		
33	faciat	et ostendas	και ποιησον
34	panem quidem hunc	panem hunc	τον μεν αρτον τουτον
35	corpus vivificans corpus salutare		
36	corpus caelest corpus liberans animas		
37	nostras et corpora		
38	corpus Domini et Dei et salvatoris	corpus venerandum Domini nostri	τιμιον σωμα
39	nostri Iesu Christi	Iesu.Christi	του Χριστου σου

e) AC's use of *apophene* seems to correspond to ATA's ostendas and may well therefore be the original verb.

d) In contrast to the elaborate style of AC in many places, the descriptions of the consecrated elements is very unembellished, agreeing with both ATA and LJC, and in marked contrast to the much fuller terminology of Sy-Jas and Byz-Basil.

e) Attention has already been drawn in Part I to the fact that the forgiveness of sins is the first of the fruits of communion common to both ATA and LJC. Precisely the same is true of AC (F61). This strengthens the likelihood of the hypothesis discussed above that in the parent anaphora the Institution Narrative ended with the phrase 'for the forgiveness of sins', which, after the briefest of linking Anamneses (which AC may now provide us with) proceeded with a request for the transforming power of the Holy Spirit on the elements, primarily for the purpose of the forgiveness of sins.

f) The closing phrases of ATA's Epiclesis, which LJC omits entirely, are not closely paralleled in AC, but what may be faint echoes are discernible. The idea of being *worthy* (F79) is present in both, as is the theme of *life*, though in ATA it is the believers' temporal life, while in AC it is eternal life (F82). Clearly, it is impossible to say more than that an ending such as found in ATA might have influenced the choice of motifs in the mind of the Redactor of AC.

Epiclesis

	Sy-Jas	ATA	LJC
40			
41			
42	in remissionem peccatorum et in vitam		μεταβαλλων τω πνευματι σου τω αγιω. Αμ
43	aeternam accipientibus. Amen.		
44	et mixtum quod in calice hoc	et calicem hunc	το δε εν τω ποτηριω τουτω
45	faciat		
46	sanguinem novi testamenti sanguinem		
47	salutarem sanguinem vivificantem		
48	sanguinem caelestem sanguinem liberantem		
49	animas nostras et corpora		
50	sanguinem	sanguinem	τιμιον αιμα
51	Domini et Dei et salvatoris nostri	Domini nostri	
52	Iesu Christi	Iesu Christi	του Χριστου σου
53			
54			μεταβαλων τω πνευματι σου τω αγιω. Αμην
55	in remissionem peccatorum		
56	et in vitam aeternam accipientibus. Amen.		
57	ut fiant omnibus ex eis accipientibus	ut sint omnibus qui de illis sumunt	ωστε γενεσθαι τοις μεταλαμβανουσιν
58			
59			εις νηψιν ψυχης
60		ad vitam et resurrectionem	
61		et remissionem peccatorum	εις αφεσιν αμαρτιων
62			
63			
64			
65			εις κοινωνιαν του αγιου σου πνευματος,
66			εις βασιλειας πληρωμα
67	in sanctitatem animarum et corporum	in sanitatem animae et corporis	
68		et illuminationem mentis	
69		et apologiam ante tribunal terribile	εις παρρησιαν την προς σε
70		Christi tui	
71			μη εις κριμα η εις κατακριμα
72			
73			
74			
75			
76			
77			
78		et nemo pereat de populo tuo Domine	
79		sed fac dignos nos omnes	
80		qui sine turbatione servientes	
81		et ministrantes	
82		ante te omni tempore vitae nostrae	
83			
84		fruamur mysteriis tuis caelestibus et	
85		immortalibus et vivificantibus per	
86		gratiam et misericordiam et philanthropiam	
87		tuam nunc....	
88	in productionem fructuum operum bonorum		
89	in confirmationem ecclesiae tuae sanctae		
90	quam fundasti supra petram fidei et		
91	portaw inferi non superabunt eam liberans		
92	eam ab omnibus haeresibus et a scandalis		
93	operantium iniquitates usque ad consumm-		
94	ationem saeculi in saecula saeculorum.		
95	Amen.		

Byz-Basil		AC
40	αυτο το τιμιον σωμα	σωμα
41	του κυριου και θεου και σωτηρος ημων	του Χριστου σου
42	Ιησου Χριστου. Αμην.	
43		
44		
45		
46	το δε ποτηριον τουτο	
47		
48		
49		
50	αυτο το τιμιον αιμα	αιμα
51	του κυριου και θεου και σωτηρος ημων	
52	Ιησου Χριστου.	του Χριστου σου
53	το εκχυθεν υπερ της του κοσμου ζωης	
54		
55		
56		
57		ινα οι μεταλαβοντες
58		βεβαιωθωσιν προς ευσεβειαν
59		
60		
61		αφεσιν αμαρτηματων τυχωσιν
62	ημας δε παντες τους εκ του ενος αρτου	
63	και του ποτηριου μετεχοντας ενωσαι	
64	αλληλοις	
65	εις ενος πνευματος αγιου κοινωνιαν	
66		
67		
68		
69	και μηδενα ημω.	
70		
71	εις κριμα η εις κατακριμα	
72	μετασχειν του αγιου σωματος και αιματος	
73	του Χριστου σου αλλ' ινα ευρωμεν ελεον και	
74	χαριν μετα παντων των αγιων των απ'αιωνος	
75	ευαρεστησαντων: προπατερων πατερων....	
76		του διαβολου και της πλανης αυτου ρυσθωσιν
77		πνευματος αγιου πληρωθωσιν
78		
79		αξιοι του Χριστου σου γενωνται
80		
81		
82		ζωης αιωνιου τυχωσιν
83		σου καταλλαγεντος αυτοις δεσποτα παντοκρατορ
84		
85		
86		
87		
88		
89		
90		
91		
92		
93		
94		
95		

Part 2 31

2G INTERCESSIONS

We have already shown that, like the Oblation, ATA and LJC have had to derive their Anaphoral Intercessions from other sources. Two main points may be said about the Intercession sequence of AC:

a) It does not correspond in basic structure with that of Byz-Basil or LJC. Although there is some dislocation of the petitions for the saints and departed (K,N,O), there is no radical reversal of the living/dead sequence.

Table G

	Sy-Jas		ATA		LJC
1	Holy Places		all men	K	patriarchs, etc.
A	the catholic Church	A	your catholic Church	L	Mary
B	the bishops	B	the bishops	f	John the Baptist
C	our bishops	a	the celebrant	M	benefit from saints'
D	presbyterate and diaconate	D	presbyters and deacons		prayers
E	other ministers		the orthodox of every land	N	the departed
a	the celebrant	G	all your faithful people	P	rest
4	deliverance from wrath		safe-keeping of your flock	B	the episcopate
b	present and absent	H	this holy church	D	presbyters and deacons
J	the offerers		every town and district of	E	other ministries
g	reward of joy, etc.		faithful		whole world
e	the emperor	I	weather and fruits	A	the catholic church
5	aged and weak	G	afflicted brethren	F	virgins
I	weather and fruits	J	the offerers	e	the emperor
K	the 'well-pleasing' saints	N	departed fathers and	H	this city and its faithful
f	John the Baptist		brothers	C	our archbishop
L	Mary	L	Mary		
g	all the saints	K	the 'well-pleasing' saints		
14	numbering with the	M	benefits from saints'		
	faithful		prayer		
22	bishops of Jerusalem				
M	benefits from saints'				
	prayers				
N	departed clergy				
O	departed laity				
P	rest with Patriarchs				
Q	preservation, guidance, etc				

b) The sequence looks more like a re-working of the ATA schema. There is a trace of a basic alphabetical sequence of the major petitions which has been dislocated by the insertion of other material. In particular the ABaD opening pattern provides and exact match with ATA, which raises the interesting possibility that the Redactor of AC may have been working not with the original parent form (which we have argued did not have anaphoral intercessions), but with a 'proto-ATA' prayer. This would imply that LJC had 'branched off' before the production of AC.

Intercessions

Byz-Basil

K the 'well-pleasing' saints
L Mary
f John the Baptist
g all the saints
M benefits from saints' prayers
N the departed
P rest with Patriarchs
A universal church
J the offerers
c heavenly recompense
F virgins
e the emperor
b those who stand by us
J scattered and wanderers
d widows and orphans
G all your faithful people
H this flock
C our bishop
B the episcopate
a the celebrant
D presbyterate and diaconate
E every order of clergy
I weather and fruits
h cessation of schism, etc.
Q preservation, guidance, etc.

AC

A your holy Church
B the bishops
a the celebrant
D presbyters, deacons and all clergy
e the emperor
K the 'well-pleasing' saints
G this people
F virgins
B married, childbearing and infants
H this city
6 afflicted brethren
  our persecutors
  catechumens
5 possessed and penitent
I weather and fruits
b the absent
Q preservation and guidance

CONCLUSIONS

1) The comparison of ATA and LJC in Part I suggested that the ancestral form had the structure: Preface—Pre-Sanctus—Sanctus—Post-Sanctus—Institution Narrative—Epiclesis, with only the briefest anamnetic link between Institution Narrative and Epiclesis. When the large blocks of descriptive material (located mainly in the Preface and Post-Sanctus) are dissected away from AC, the remaining material shows a significant number of points of similarity in structure, content and wording in precisely those sections which we have identified as belonging to the ATA/LJC ancestral form. Despite the massive re-working which AC has undergone, characteristic phrases, not found in Sy-Jas or LJC (eg D4-7, E1-6, F61) are found in all three texts. The lack of agreement in the Oblation and (with the qualification noted above) in the Intercession corroborates the ATA/LJC evidence as to the parent structure.

It seems possible to assert, therefore, that AC, ATA and LJC represent three independent re-workings of an original anaphora. ATA and LJC have been created by conflation with material from Sy-Jas and Byz-Basil respectively. AC has been created by greatly expanding the original core, with large amounts of rhetorical and biblical material, and with liturgical material derived from other prayers. Nevertheless, the Redactor has been unwilling to discard some of the characteristic phrases of his original, which survive at various points and in particular in the 'false' Pre-Sanctus and Anamnesis.

2) The findings relating to the missing Oblation merit further comment.

As Table E shows, the only certain trace of material in the ATA/LJC Anamnesis position is the line 'We, therefore, remembering this saving commandment and all the things that were done for us' (E1-6). This *might* have been followed from the very beginning by a list of 'the things that were done for us' (and if it wasn't, it certainly provided an irresistable cue line for a later Redactor), but it gives us no help with the existence of an oblation. The 'saving commandment' referred to may not be to 'do this', which does not of course occur in the LJC text, but to the 'eat' and 'drink' in the Dominical Words. But could an anaphora proceed from Narrative to closing Epiclesis?

Parallels with texts ending with a closing petition at the end of the Epiclesis are not in fact hard to find and some have been indicated above.

This is in fact what Ap Trad does, with only a simple one-sentence Anamnesis/oblation. The Deir Balyzeh Papyrus looks as though it is about to proceed directly from Institution Narrative to petition (?for the Holy Spirit) and certainly concludes with a general petition and congregational Amen. The anaphora of St Mark, though not having the Institution Narrative/Epiclesis link, nevertheless still testifies to the possibility of ending an anaphora with an Epiclesis and petition for fruitful communion. Cyril of Jerusalem's anaphora, of course, moved straight from Sanctus to Epiclesis, thus demonstrating that an invocation of the Holy Spirit does not invariably have to follow an Anamnesis.

But is it possible that an Epiclesis might follow directly on an Institution Narrative with perhaps only the briefest of links? The clue here seems to be provided by the 'false' Anamnesis of AC, when considered in relation to the text of the LJC Institution Narrative. This latter is quite terse, particularly in the Dominical Words and lacks the additional features found in the other rites under examination. In particular, there is no 'do this in remembrance of me' or citation of 1 Cor. 11. (ATA has almost certainly followed Sy-Jas here, while LJC has declined to copy Byz-Basil.) If we follow LJC's Narrative with ATA's Epiclesis, linking them with AC's 'false' Anamnesis (slightly re-arranged in ATA/LJC sequence) we get a smooth flow:

'. . . Drink from this all of you; this is my blood of the new Covenant, which is shed for you and for many for the forgiveness of sins'. We, therefore, remembering this saving commandment and all the things that were done for us, give you thanks, almighty God, and ask that you send your Holy Spirit upon the offerings set before you, and show *this* bread to be the venerated body of our Lord Jesus Christ, and *this* cup the blood of our Lord Jesus Christ, that they may be to all who partake of them for *for forgiveness of sins*, and boldness . . .'

If this were the original text, it would explain

a) the alleged lack of an anamnesis in Chrysostom's writings;

b) the fact that no trace of an 'ancestral' oblation is detectable in ATA, LJC or AC, and that instead all three seem to have borrowed one from three different sources;

c) the apparent reluctance of the Redactor of ATA to put an oblation into his conflated anaphora.

The present Study claims to be merely a preliminary investigation. Clearly further work needs to be done:

a) to elucidate further the precise form of the texts that influenced the various Redactors;

b) to reconstruct the ancestral form of the anaphora and to investigate its relationship to what is already known of the primitive prayer of Antioch.

c) to elucidate the location, date and language of the various stages of reworking.

Doubtless some modifications of the present paper will emerge (for example, there are grounds for believing that the text that influenced ATA was not Sy-Jas as we now have it, but an earlier stage, perhaps closer to Gk-Jas), but the evidence presented above would seem to take us one step closer to the origins of the highly influential family of West Syrian anaphoras.

---

[1] If AC's 'false Anamnesis' in fact retains the original verb ('we therefore *fulfilling* his command' and remembering all the things . . .), the flow is, if anything, even more satisfactory.

[2] Using terms defined by the author in previous studies. See Fenwick, *op. cit.*

Alcuin/GROW Joint Liturgical Studies

All cost £3.25 (US $7) in 1990

1987 TITLES

1. **(LS 49) Daily and Weekly Worship—from Jewish to Christian**
   by Roger Beckwith, Warden of Latimer House, Oxford

2. **(LS 50) The Canons of Hippolytus**
   edited by Paul Bradshaw, Professor of Liturgics, University of Notre Dame

3. **(LS 51) Modern Anglican Ordination Rites**
   edited by Colin Buchanan, then Bishop of Aston

4. **(LS 52) Models of Liturgical Theology**
   by James Empereur, of the Jesuit School of Theology, Berkeley

1988 TITLES

5. **(LS 53) A Kingdom of Priests: Liturgical Formation of the Laity: The Brixen Essays**
   edited by Thomas Talley, Professor of Liturgics, General Theological Seminary, New York.

6. **(LS 54) The Bishop in Liturgy: an Anglican Study**
   edited by Colin Buchanan, then Bishop of Aston

7. **(LS 55) Inculturation: the Eucharist in Africa**
   by Phillip Tovey, research student, previously tutor in liturgy in Uganda

8. **(LS 56) Essays in Early Eastern Initiation**
   edited by Paul Bradshaw, Professor of Liturgics, University of Notre Dame

1989 TITLES

9. **(LS 57) The Liturgy of the Church in Jerusalem**
   by John Baldovin

10. **(LS 58) Adult Initiation**
    edited by Donald Withey

11. **(LS 59) 'The Missing Oblation': The Contents of the Early Antiochene Anaphora**
    by John Fenwick

12. **(LS 60) Calvin and Bullinger on the Lord's Supper**
    by Paul Rorem

1990 TITLES

13-14 **(LS 61/62) The Liturgical Portions of The Apostolic Constitutions: A Text for Students**
   edited by W. Jardine Grisbrooke (March 1990)
   This double-size volume provides in effect two of the Studies for 1990, and costs double price (i.e. £6.50 in England in 1990).

15. **(LS 63) Liturgical Inculturation in the Anglican Communion**
    edited by David Holeton, Professor of Liturgics, Trinity College, Toronto (June 1990)
    The Anglican International Liturgical Consultation at York in August 1989 adopted a major statement on liturgical inculturation. 'Down to Earth Worship'. This symposium reprints the Statement and expounds it and applies it to various parts of the Anglican Communion. It is published early, following no. 13-14, in order to be available to the ACC in 1990.

16. **(LS64) Cremation Today and Tomorrow**
    by Douglas Davies, University of Nottingham (December 1990)
    A practical study of attitudes towards cremation, with theological suggestions for new cremation services.

Grove Liturgical Studies

This series began in March 1975, and was published quarterly until 1986. Nos. 1, 3-6, 10 and 30 are out of print. Asterisked numbers have been reprinted. Prices in 1990, £2.50

Previous Alcuin titles

(obtainable through booksellers, or via Grove Books Limited, post-free).

1980 *The Communion of Saints* (by Michael Perham) S.P.C.K. £6.95

1981 *Daily Prayer in the Early Church* (by Paul Bradshaw) S.P.C.K. £6.95

1982 *Nuptial Blessing* (by Kenneth Stevenson) S.P.C.K. £10.50

1983 *The Godly Order* (by Geoffrey Cuming) S.P.C.K. £8.50

1984 *Latest Anglican Liturgies 1976-1984* (edited by Colin Buchanan) S.P.C.K. (hardback) (reduced price) £6.50.

1985 *The Meaning of Baptism* (by Raymond Burnish) S.P.C.K. £10.50

1986 *Earth and Altar* (by Donald Gray) Canterbury Press £10.50

Also 'Alcuin Club Manuals'

No. 1 *The Eucharist* (by Michael Perham) S.P.C.K. 1981, £2.25

No. 3 *Family Services* (by Kenneth Stevenson) S.P.C.K., 1981, £2.25

The Alcuin Club

Membership of the Alcuin Club includes the cost of the four Joint Liturgical Studies each year within the annual subscription rate, on a reduced basis, Details from

> The Rev. Tim Barker
> 6 Hillfield
> Norton
> Runcorn
> Cheshire WA7 6RN

(Address after April 1990):

> All Saints Vicarage
> Highlands Avenue
> Runcorn
> Cheshire WA7 4PS